MERCUTIO & HIS BROTHER VALENTINE

A Play by Clayton Garrett

Robert Elliot and Graham Banville. Photo by John Geddes

Mercutio & His Brother Valentine was first produced by Impromptu Productions on April 19, 2013 in Kingston, Ontario. It was performed in repertory with Romeo & Juliet under the direction of Matthew Davis. The cast was as follows:

Valentine...Robert Elliott

Mercutio...Graham Banville

Rosaline...Signy Lynch

Prince Escalus.......................................John Geddes

Friar Lawrence...................................Mitch Nasheim

Benvolio..Radissen Ramoutar

Capulet...John Farant

Tybalt...Ben Hudson

Paris...Christopher Ormrod

Peter..Matthew MacDonald

Romeo..Ryan Armstrong

Juliet...Jennifer Verardi

Servants.......Derek Liston, Loren Smith, Hayley Hudson

Nurse..Hilary Taynen

Lady Capulet..Sue Del-Mei

The play was performed with one 15 minute intermission.

MERCUTIO & HIS BROTHER VALENTINE

ACT ONE

The following action takes place within Romeo and Juliet between Act I Sc II and concludes just after Act III Sc III. Valentine a younger man is in his study. There is a large stained glass window up stage behind the large desk the window is made up of various colours of glass. His desk is covered with loose papers, parchments and books of various sizes. Books and documents are staked on the floor around the rooms. An easel stands in the corner and a half finished sculpture of a nude male sits beside it. There is one entrance to the room stage right. From the look of the room a real renaissance man lives here. He goes to the bookshelf and selects a book. Then goes over to a scientific experiment he is working on.

Val: Now what have we here?

Consulting his book he lights a candle. Valentine holds a gold piece in his tongs to the candle flame for a few seconds then starts to write observations in a note book.

Val: The amount of fire required to have a given amount of gold change its state is great and less than perfect. I would argue the assumption that gold is the most perfect of all metals is false. That due only to notions of material gain, is this fallacy perpetuated.

He then takes a bit of another metal in the end of his tongs.

Val: Of all the metals and salts in the known world none, in my estimation, none are truer to the pure state than this salt I obtained from a Greek. It appears no different than many others, tin or silver, but it has one slight difference that is revealed by fire, and small amount of flame.

He then touches that to the flame causing it to ignite and burn brightly then winks out.

Val : The material ignites and burns brighter, hotter and more intense. More brilliant than the original source, but for a far shorter time until it is totally consumed, leaving only the smallest amount of ash. Perfection. However for this material reaching that state of perfection, even only briefly, it owes everything to that which forced it to change its state. The catalyst or the original flame. Without it, there would be no perfection and it would remain imperfect forever.

Valentine blows out the candle and sets it to the side knocking some parchments and a letter on the floor. He seems not to notice.. Valentine seems pleased with these results and puts his experiments to the side. He then looks through his clutter till he finds a book. The door flies open and Mercutio runs in and slams it shut behind. Leaning on the door for a second looks around wildly, Val seems not to notice and continues reading. Mercutio starts searching the room looking for something.

Mer: Knock, knock good brother. You're not sleeping I trust? Ah no, as I suspected. His nose in a book.

Val: What do you have against reading?

Mer: It's a waste of time.

Val : Not if one knows how to read, it takes not any time at all.

Mer: What are you reading?

Val: Summa Perfectionis. One of the oldest and rarest books on the study of Alchemy....

Mer: Fascinating. No really. You want to talk about old books, I once saw a book from the east and there were pictures of men and women in the most interesting of positions. Kama… Kama something? You should really read that one.

Val: Is there not a Tavern open?

Mer: No. Well maybe, what time is it? Never mind it matters not, I shall not darken the door of any tavern this night.

Val: Oh, what's the occasion? Is it Lent already? (Gets up to pour more wine.)

Mer: Oh no my good brother, for tonight we drink for free!

Val: We?

Mer: We, are invited to the feast of the Capulet's. Here's your invitation. (He hands Val a letter.)

Val: Harrah. Just put it in that basket there beside you.

Mer: You don't even want to read it?

Val: No.

Mer: Awe come on, Capulet went to a lot of trouble to get you this invite and you are just going to throw it away?

Val: I'm not in the mood Mercutio. Throw it in the basket.

Mer: The basket needs to be emptied.

Val: Just throw it on the floor then.

Mer: You know you could have someone tidy up a little in here?

Val: Things are fine the way they are I know exactly where everything is.

Mer: No really that's why the Prince has all these people running around in the palace all the time… you may have seen them? They all go around wearing the same clothing and constantly say "My lord" whenever you speak to one.

Mer: (Finding a letter on the floor begins reading.) Dearest Father, I am writing you with regards to our conversation as of last August in this year of our Lord, where I expressed to you my interest in a position in your Jesuit brotherhood.

Val: Give that here!

Mer: So it's the Jesuits?

Val: None of your concern Mercutio.

Mer: My brother a Jesuit?

Val: Yes if you must know, I have decided I like their order.

Mer: But won't they send you to the new world or some forsaken place?

Val: Yes, with some luck.

Knock at the door. Mercutio now very hastily squeezes into the spot he cleared out under the desk.

Val: (Val opens the door.) Yes?

Ser: Sorry to bother you my lord Valentine, but Lord Escalus and my master the Stewart are seeking the lord Mercutio.

Valentine is standing where he can see the servant and Mercutio,
Mercutio he glares at Mercutio who just smiles and shrugs.

Val: Have you tried looking under the furniture?

Ser: My lord?

Val: I have not seen him.

Ser: Thank you my lord.

Servant leaves and closes the door.

Mer: The head steward is mad again I'm afraid.

Val: His daughter?

Mer: She was caught sneaking in last night. Or this
morning more the like I guess.

Val: You must really leave that man's daughter alone
Mercutio.

Mer: It's hard to. She's so... well you've seen her! Oh
but it must be easy for you, you're a priest.

Val: Not yet, which is a good thing. With you having
me lying to the servants all the time.

Mer: It's not "all the time". But for this you have my
thanks brother. (Pouring a drink) You know this
place really is a stable, books and parchment
strewn all about I've seen neater brothels and
believe me, I've seen my brothels!

Val : Why have you come here? To hide under my
furniture and tell me I live a pig's life?

Mer: Aren't we sensitive? Apologies. Dearest brother
you are not a pig. And if you have it in your heart
to forgive me my insensitivities I'm sure I can
repay my transgressions, and all will be forgotten
when you join us for a drink at the feast tonight.

Val: Us? Who is "us"?

Mer: The lads and I.

Val: Who?

Mer: You know. The lads.

Val: Tell me he's not going go there.

Mer: He is one of the lads.

Val: Are you all mad?

Mer: What?

Val: He'll be killed. You'll all be killed for sure, simply for being there with him.

Mer: Relax good brother, we will be fine. It is a masquerade!

Val: Back less than a fortnight and up to trouble!

Mer: You really are ready to start preaching aren't you father-brother?

Val: Mercutio use your head. Convince that fool Montague to stay home tonight.

Mer: I told you it is a masquerade. There will be so many there, no one will know the difference. All will be shrouded in Beetle Brows.

Val: I see you are to be going as a fool.

Mer: Your originality astounds me.

Val : How is it that "The Lads", as you put it, are even going to get in? I trust it is by invite only.

Mer: There, that's a beauty. The servant who was entrusted with delivery of the invites, Peter or something, apparently is not a very skilled reader. Not my first choice for such a task, but there you are. By the way, yours is addressed to some Venetian merchant by the name of Shylock?

Val: I'm not going.

Mer: Nonsense, it will be fun! All the finest ladies of Verona will be in attendance; you may even get lucky.

Val: I'm perfectly lucky as it is, and I can have as much fun as I need to right here thanks. If you call dodging Capulet blades fun that is.

Mer: Carving miniatures of naked men? Come on.

Val: No.

Mer: Are you coming?

Val: No I'm not.

Mer: Come on Val, you need to get out. How long has it been since you danced?

Val: I don't dance.

Mer: Yes you do.

Val: I do no such thing!

Mer: You do too.

Val: Mercutio, I'm not going to argue with you about this. I don't dance.

Mer: You used to.

Val: I <u>used</u> to. I don't now.

Mer: What have you got against dancing?

Val: Nothing. It's just not for me, it serves no purpose.

Mer: Sure it does, many a lass has lost her resolve to me and I owe it all to my saucy moves.

Val : Well there, that's one of the many differences between us.

Mer: Spoken like a fine monk of the brotherhood.

Val : Grazie.

Mer: You know father-brother, aside from merriment there is no purpose. See that's the problem with you Valentine, everything has to have some big purpose. Some big "reason why." Why can't you just accept that there are some things we do simply for no reason at all, only because it feels good? That life is so long and dismal, we invent things like dancing to pass the time and make it go along quicker.

Val: I read.

Mer: Well mother's lock your daughter's up! Valentine's got a book!

Val: That's what it all comes down to with you isn't it?

Mer: Not always. I also like to fight... and drink.

Val: You're hopeless.

Mer: Don't you ever get bored just reading about other men's adventures? Haven't you ever wanted to make some adventure of you own?

Val: Why, when I can live vicariously through you?

Mer: I'm serious, don't you wish you could hunt for the grail or the golden fleece?

Val: This is the modern age there are no more Arthur's or Jason's. And just because you and your friends drink, fight and fornicate. That doesn't mean you all will be immortalized in word, song or stone.

Mer: That's how it works for a soldier.

Val: And you would still have a career if you stayed there.

Mer: Do you always have to be such a villain? I came here to see if you would like to come to a nice banquet and you use it as an opportunity to dig at me.

Val: Now who's sensitive? I'm not digging at you.

Mer: You are too but you know what Val? I don't care, I'm happy and you're not,.simple as that. And that really chaps you where the sun never tans.

Val: You must admit you had it pretty good in the army. Escalus offered you a command and you threw it in his face.

Mer: That was something our good cousin Escalus decided for me. You think it's so sweet you can have it.

Val: If a career in the military suited me, I would.

Mer: What makes you think it suits me?

Val: You have no interest in studies or the church, what else is a gentleman with no rank or titles going to do? The army can open a lot of doors.

Mer: A door that can come back only to slam your toes. I had no say. I tried it; I hated it, so that's the end of it.

Val: Fine.

Mer: (Pause) Are you coming tonight or not?

Val: I am not.

Mer: Fine. (Long pause) I don't think I want you anyway. You'd just try to make me feel guilty if I were having any fun.

Val: Probably.

Mer: (Even longer pause) So what should I say to people?

Val: What do you mean?

Mer: When they ask where you are?

Val: I don't care.

Mer: How about, "Valentine? Oh I'm afraid he couldn't make it, he's been hitting the bottle pretty hard lately and the family thought it best if he stayed out of public view."

Val: I don't care.

Mer: Or "No I'm afraid he couldn't make it tonight he's ill, he's been spending a lot of time down at the docks lately and seems to be suffering from an itchy burning rash down around his..."

Val: Mercutio!

Mer: "He must have got more than he'd paid for from a dirty little wharf wench."

Val: Mercutio! Will you cork it? I'm not going so that's the end of it.

Mer: All right but I'm not going to be responsible for what might come out of my mouth.

Val: Why should tonight be any different?

Mer I get nervous sometimes when strangers ask me personal questions, and who knows what I might blurt out?

Val: I don't care what you tell people. Nobody would believe a word from your mouth anyway.

Mer: Yes, most don't. But the good Friar Lawrence did that time back, you remember?

Val: I remember. I could have killed you.

Mer: Capulets feast, the last time you went years ago!

Val: You stole the friar's herbs!

Mer: That grayish-green stuff, you told me he said it was never to be mixed with vinegar and ingested.

Val: Because it is intoxicating.

Mer: We put nearly a full dram into that bottle of vinegar and drank all night. We were gloriously drunk!

Val: I have never in my life been as sick that next day.

Mer: Oh but there has never been a night more worth it! If Signor Placentio had any idea what went on with his nieces we'd both be dead for sure.

Val: I had nothing to do with that, you were the one who plied them with that hateful concoction.

Mer: They were curious. I merely satisfied their curiosity about that, and many other things as well that night.

Val: The Friar was going to have us hanged, he was sure one of us had stolen his herbs. But then you told him that story about his basket falling down the well while he was dancing.

Mer: The Friar has been at many festivals and gets so in his humours that I don't think he can remember one from another.

Val:I could not believe you stole, and then lied to a man of the cloth.

Mer: I didn't lie. There was some truth. The basket did fall down the well, once. It's the fine art of crafting a good tale using bits of truth to keep ones head from the chopping block.

Val: Well it did save our heads for sure.

Mer: I remember when you were fun.

Val: He is not really going to the Capulets Feast tonight, is he?

Mer: Yes.

Val: You're not leading me on now?

Mer: We're all going together, you should come.

Val: Why on earth would a Montague possibly want to go to a Capulet party? I mean just this morning I heard all hell broke forth; the watch had a devil of a time breaking it up I hear. That's thrice this has happened. Come to think of it, you weren't there were you?

Mer: No, no. I missed it all unfortunately. Head Steward's daughter? You want to know why he's going?

Val: Let me guess... a girl?

Mer: Right on the nose brother!

Val: That lad would follow his codpiece into a volcano. Who is she now?

Mer: None other than young lady Rosaline.

Val: Do I know her?

Mer: I doubt it, I haven't even met her.

Val: Does he have a chance?

Mer: Not in the slightest.

Val: Too bad he's going to throw himself on a Capulet sword then.

Mer: It is. You know though, it was all Tybalt's fault. I mean that brawl earlier this morning, Benvolio told me how it came about.

Val: I'm sure Benvolio behaved like the model subject Escalus would expect in the given the situation.

Mer: I've let a lot of things go between Tybalt and myself, because of my loyalty to our cousin. But mark me, one day Tybalt and I are going to come to blows and I'll put my foot so far in his back side, I'll need a surgeon for a cobbler.

Val: Careful I hear he's very good.

Mer: I'm better.

Val: They say he's the best in Verona.

Mer: (Mocking.) They say he's the best in Verona…

Val: Tybalt's family has paid very well to have him study with the best masters.

Mer: I'm better.

Val: (Patronizingly.) I know you are.

Mer: You want to have a go? I see a couple of old foils here covered in dust and rust. Were these our dead grandfathers? No, I would think not, he knew how to take care of a blade.

Val: Sure. But some other time Mercutio.

Mer: No how about now?

Val: Later.

Mer: You can't just walk away now brother. Come, back up what you say.

Val: No really, I'm sorry I brought it all up.

Mer: No you don't, take the foil.

Val: I don't know, you with that army training of yours...?

Mer: Ah ha! I knew it, you are afraid to lose. You always hated losing.

Val: ...I don't want to embarrass the Prince's militia.

Mer: Take the blasted foil.

Val: Mercutio I'm not going to…

Mer: Here… Take it.

Val: No.

Mer: Take it!

Val: And then you leave?

Mer: Yes, take it.

Val: Fine! Fine! If it means you will leave me in peace.

Mer: Best two out of three?

They fight playfully at first then progressively more intense.
Valentine hits.

Val: One!

Mer: Luck.

They fight again. Valentine hits.

Val: Two! I win!

Mer: Three out of five!

Val: How many times have I heard you say that? You always do that when I get two out of three. Three out of five, five out seven. No I'm done now goodbye. (Mercutio hits Valentine hard.) Oww!

Mer: One for me!

Val: I wasn't ready.

Mer: And the sun was in your eyes as well I'd suppose?

Mercutio hits.

Mer: Two we're tied!

Valentine is visibly angry by the force Mercutio has been using. They fight again and the fight intensifies now. Both men seem to be quite challenged.

Mercutio hits.

Mer: Ha! And soldiers everywhere come along with their honor intact! Five out of seven?

Valentine lunges for Mercutio throwing rapiers aside. The two men grapple for a time with Mercutio laughing the whole while. Val realizes he has lost it a bit, embarrassed he and breaks it off.

Mer: Hold steady there brother, it was just a bit of fun.

Val: Indeed. Now that you have had it, it's time for you to go. That was the bargain.

Mer: It's just a bit of horseplay there is no need.

Val I have work to do.

Mer: I'm not leaving till you get yourself ready for the Capulet feast.

Val: I told you I'm not going, now leave me be! Get out!

Mer: Whatever then. Throws the sword.

Knock at door.

Val: Come!

Enter Friar Lawrence with a basil plant.

Mer: Friar Lawrence love to chat but alas I was just leaving it seems.

Law: Benedictae young Mercutio I've missed you at mass this last little while?

Mer: Yes well, I've been finding it difficult to make it to Sunday morning mass. You see strangest thing, every week at that same time on that same day I awake to find I'm violently ill. Headaches, vomiting, loud noises bother me especially.

Law: That is wondrous strange, have you had a doctor look to it?

Mer: No, they would just try to put leeches on me or some such thing. I don't believe in them. Doctors that is.

Law: You know there are other masses, ones that begin later in the day. Masses that others who suffer from the same affliction as yours can attend?

Mer: Yes well, right then. I shall have to look to it father, grazia.

Law: Dominus vobiscum, my son.

      Mercutio exits.

Val: Why do you do that?

Law: Do what?

Val: Indulge him, play his fool?

Law: I am no fool Valentine, not for your brother or anyone. Mercutio and I play a game that is all.

Val: I'm sorry father, but I'm just sick to death of playing Mercutio's games.

Law: Your man said you'd be in here, if this is a bad time...?

Val: It's not a problem Friar. My apologies, it's just that my visits with him sometimes can leave me somewhat on edge.

Law: I have not seen him much since he returned. The truth is, he does not come to Mass as often as he should.

Val: You know Mercutio, he never does what he should do.

Law: I love Mercutio as much as I you Valentine. But there is a difference as to my expectations. For him, they are never set so high your brother can't meet them, therefore he rarely disappoints me.

Val: That is the problem, everyone lets him away with things that the rest of us are not ever allowed to be excused from.

Law: True, it might be a little unfair some times I would think. But he has spirit and is prone to wilder ways. It's best to let him find his own way and not to force him, in my opinion.

Val: He has spirit enough to get himself killed on a Capulet blade unless he starts learning something about limitations.

Law: True again my good Valentine. It is important for all men of Verona to be mindful of the dangers that lurk in these streets. It is not good to get betwixed Capulets and Montagues. But Mercutio's resourcefulness I really quite admire. A very great asset to him I would say.

Val: His resourcefulness gets him into as many troubles as it saves him from.

Law: Too true. That time with my herbs should come to mind.

Val: He's still very proud of that ruse. And to be honest, you only knew the truth of what happened because I told you during my confession.

Law: Which sadly is the reason why I can never catch him up. You will learn as you start your work to hearing confessions there are sometimes certain frustrations we are bound to bear. This is one of mine. I brought you a gift, one of my plants.

Val: You shouldn't have.

Law: It was no trouble. It is a basil, I thought you might like an herb plant.

Val: Indeed it's wonderful. Thank you.

Law: Everything is well I trust?

Val: Well enough.

Law: Excellent. Valentine, I hope you don't mind but I have taken the liberty of contacting some of the brothers at the seminary on your behalf. There seems to be a great deal of interest in the prospect of your entry. Father John of Mantua was very impressed by you and he ranks high with our order.

Val: Wine father?

Law: Oh I shouldn't I've got so much to do.

Val: Would you mind if I do?

Law: No please...

He watches Val pour a glass

Law: You might just as well go ahead and pour me a little smell. I can't stand to see a man drink alone, it wouldn't be proper.

Val: Of course.

Law: Many more fields of study are available now than when I attended seminary, of course that was ages ago. Truth is not much has changed in my field, the use of herbs. However I do still find it as fascinating as the day I grew my first seed. (Val hands Law wine.) Bless you. (Drinks.) I know it won't be for a long time yet but have you given any thought to where you might like appointment?

Val: Yes, well sort of.

Law: One does not have much control over where the church feels you're best suited especially when you vow to go where the Holy Father sends, but you do have a preference?

Val: A missionary post might be intriguing I suppose. See the new world. Father the thing is, I've been thinking very hard about this and I'm not sure how to say this but, think I would quite like to travel after my studies. Maybe find a quiet appointment where I can do my work.

Law: Oh…

Val: I would really like to concentrate on alchemy as my choice of study. And it would seem, I have found, that the Jesuit Order is more of a better suit for me than your Franciscan Brotherhood.

Law: The Jesuits? They do have better facilities than our Franciscans, newer schools, but a much longer process to gain the cloth you know.

Val: I know but I'm not worried about time. There will always be a missionary post until the whole world is discovered.

Law: Well I'm sure the world could use a wise young man, like yourself, my son to bring the word into the darkness. But I'm even more sure that this same young man is of more importance here at home.

Val: What do you mean Father?

Law: Verona cries out in suffering, the Prince's own kinsman as their shepherd would be the very thing that would bring healing to this wounded flock.

Val: I'm not sure I see what your suggesting Father.

Law: Valentine I have been at this parish for so long now I almost can't remember any other home. I arrived when your brother and you were little more than babes. I was here when your parents spirits were laid to rest. But yesterday's events have me more worried than ever. A tense peace rests in Verona. Even so, I've been thinking. If Prince Escalus' own kinsman could become my successor, I see a great light in a grim future. Such closeness to the Prince's rule and Holy Church would, like a hammer and anvil forge Capulet and Montague to more peaceful ways.

Val: Father I'm flattered you think I could help these matters, but is it not up to the church to decide your successor?

Law: I'm sure Father John could carry a lot of weight in the matter. And I'm more than sure he could be persuaded to see that you are the best choice for Verona.

Val: Friar as my friend and mentor I'm elated you think so highly of my potential. But as my priest and confessor I must tell you I don't think I can do any better job making peace in Verona.

Law: Think Valentine. Your cousin Escalus stands on the law of Verona. You can stand with the Holy Church of Rome at your back, the Pope himself, the man with the very keys to heaven itself behind you. You would be his voice in Verona. Such a marriage of church and state unlike any other. Every Sunday the souls gather at the parish and the aisle in the pews draw a solid line between rivals. Some of my parishioners too afraid to come to mass, they fear they may sit and accidently align themselves on one side of the feud or the other. But you, Valentine, can bridge the gap. You do not remember the days when Montague and Capulet were like brothers. But before my time is finally up I would like to see these two friends again.

Val: Why do they kill each other?

Law: Only old Montague and old Capulet would know that answer. A fathers hate is a birthright and is passed like inheritance from son to grandson. There are certain plants that one can use to heal a body. But there is no herb or poultice that can be applied to wounds such as these. I can see it is time for a new healer here. Never enough time ever. (He empties his glass.) I should be off. I'm proud of you my dear lad and you shall make a fine Father. God bless you, my son.

Val: And you father.

Friar Lawrence exits and Valentine go to his desk and looks at his letter to the Jesuits lost in thought. After a moment he folds it carefully and places it on the desk. A knock at the door. The Prince enters into the room holding a mask.

Val: My Prince. How good to see you. Forgive me I had not expected you. What brings you to my little part of the palace?

Esc: We haven't spoken much lately and I was curious to know how things were with you.

Val: Well. I have been rather busy with studies.

Esc: Alchemy?

Val: Indeed, I've been looking at properties of salts and mercury.

Esc: It would be good to see you turn out some gold.

Val: Well changing a lesser metal to purer gold is only part of the pursuit. But it does not end there. Did you know it may be possible to take a lesser metal and through process find it an even truer form? Even turn it to pure light. A state of absolute perfection. Imagine my lord, a perfection like that hasn't been seen on earth since Eden before the fall!

Esc: Indeed. You spoke with Friar Lawrence this morning?

Val: He just left.

Esc: Good. Valentine I have two things to speak with you about cousin. Firstly, when was the last time you were out of your rooms?

Val: I haven't been to mass in a while but the Friar comes by to hear my confession.

Esc: I'm not talking about mass or errands. I brought you something.

Val: A mask, that is most kind my lord. I shall hang it on the wall as...

Esc: It is not for your wall. I need you to do something for me consider it a kindness.

Val: You have been most kind to us my lord. What would you have of me?

Esc: Mercutio...

Val: My lord, you cannot expect me to be Mercutio's keeper?

Esc: Not keeper, just a friendly face from this house, should need be.

Val: What do you mean my lord?

Esc: I need someone I can trust to attend the party. If there should be any incident that might involve your brother.

Val: No… no Capulet would be fool enough to harm the Prince's cousin.

Esc: It's Mercutio harming a Capulet I worry over. Your brother drinks too much. Cousin when your father and mother died I took two young boys into this palace and did my level best to raise them as I would have had they been my own flesh and blood. I have a rule to some day bestow and you would make an excellent politician, but that is not your path. I have reconciled that Valentine will not be Prince of Verona.

Val: You mean then Mercutio? Have you spoken to him?

Esc: I set him a command in our militia hoping that would help shape him. But there I have failed. Mercutio proved to be insubordinate. Since then, Mercutio has returned I cannot say more than five words to him before we argue. I need your help Valentine, I have asked that he limit his time with the Montagues, with Romeo, for the sake of the diplomacy but he thinks I'm just trying to control him. If he were to become Prince thinking as he does now, this war would get the best of him and he would be engulfed in the flames of a burning Verona.

Val: Sure Capulet and Montague do not gauge their standing with our house based on Mercutio's closeness to Romeo?

Esc: I have had to order our lamp lighters at dusk to begin either side of Verona at the same time so as not to look like I have favour one over the other. They fixate on the smallest of details old Capulet and old Montague. Such is the depths of their rivalry.

Val: Cousin, why do they fight? The Montagues and Capulets.

Esc: There are not many in all of Verona who know that answer. Before you boys came to live here it was at one of my galas in this palace that old Capulet betrayed his best friend Montague. That night a servant summoned me to a disturbance in a room in the upper quarters of the east wing. When I arrived, Lady Montague was there disheveled, her dress torn, her hair a mess. At first I thought her to be the victim of a cowardly assault. But there too was old Capulet on his knees his best friend standing over him with his fist raised to deliver another blow. The guilty look in Capulet's eye and blood on his mouth, told the whole story. Montague was incensed and enraged, he spat curses as I held him back from killing the man who was like a brother to him. He swore then that he would one day have revenge on his friend for "turning his wife into a whore", as he put it. Once things calmed a bit we three decided it was best to handle this in as discrete a manner as possible. All these years since this has just been between these parties. I would guess not even the Lady Capulet would know of the events of that night. And the servant who directed me to the scene retired most comfortably for his efforts and the part he played. Secrets Valentine, Verona's rife with them. I'm sure in time you will learn many more as Verona's confessor.

Val: My lord, I strongly feel that the Jesuit order would be the best for all. The Jesuits offer studies and opportunities that the Franciscans are not even in touch with.

Esc: I have always felt your studies were of absolute importance. But that order cannot help us with our long-term goal.

Val: But this is not what I would choose.

Esc: The other is not where your duty lies.

Val: Am I not to have any say? No control over my destiny?

Esc There is no destiny cousin, you are the son of the regent of Verona. There is only fate here. Now get ready, you have a party to attend.

Prince exits. Valentine bows and watches him leave; he walks the desk picks up the letter and crumples it throwing it across the room. He then picks up the mask and sits. Lights fade.

ACT TWO

Capulet's feast. Mercutio, Benvolio and the lads are at one side, Romeo breaks to a with a servant.

Rom: What lady's that that doth rich the hand Of yonder knight?

Pete: I know not sir. (Exits)

Romeo wonders off and spies Juliet. As Mercutio and Benvolio are talking Romeo and Juliet are on stage doing their scene at the Capulet party Rosaline, Tybalt and Capulet are seen as well.

Ben: Where is Romeo?

Mer: Straight to Rosaline, I'd bet. Though how one could tell with such concealed company? But Romeo, with but one whiff of his loves perfume, he could find her in a dung heap in the dark.

Ben: Is that he?

Mer: With those ancient breasts?

Ben: No! Not that one, over there talking to the girl.

Mer: For sure. But that's not Rosaline, that's Old Capulet's daughter! That young dog! Look at the cannon balls on that one! Not five minutes in the door and right after old Capulet's daughter. Mark you his mask is off, Benvolio, it looks as like we may to have to save this rogue's hide.

Ben: Stand down Mercutio, none know who he is.

Mer: Tybalt can see. Look you, the way he clenches his fists and gnashes his teeth.

Ben: That's just how he always looks.

Mer: You think?

Ben: For certain. If the man weren't so constipated he would look more relaxed.

Mer: I wonder when last he had a constitutional?

Ben: Not since he entered adult life, I'd say.

Mer: That would explain much.

Ben: Let us forget them. And shall we not indulge in this feast of young ladies, I see before mine eyes?

Mer: This many young lovelies in one place, a man will feel compelled to one of two things, fight or fornicate. If it is fight my friends require I can accommodate. But if not, and then need be me to fornicate, I can as well oblige.

Ben: I am touched by your offer.

Mer: You flatter yourself to think you could win such a man as me to suit.

Ben: But to my liking, the ladies are more able to suit me than the latter.

Mer: You mean to fornicate?

Ben: For unlawful carnal knowledge yes, but not the latter no.

Mer: Judging the stature of most of the ladies here, you may need a ladder to suit.

Ben: To fornicate?

Mer: Perhaps that too.

Ben: Meaning I am short?

Mer: Inadequate.

Ben: Perhaps more than adequate where it most counts.

Mer: Counting your reputation abroad with broads, I hear you to be shortly inadequate too. I have long had reputation abroad with the broads, of one that is long and broad.

Ben: Enough words. Because of your insults, this friend now requires the fight of you.

Mer: Bring on good Benvolio! As said, I will oblige.

They begin to wrestle each other and bump rather hard into a lady with a cat mask near by.

Mer: Peace Benvolio! Good lady, I ask you your pardon. My short friend here was displaying his meager prowess...

Ben: Pardon lady, my friend here made pass at me, and feeling my honor behooved, I needed to explain Benvolio is woman to no man...

Ros: You both are forgiven, if you would do of me but one favour.

Mer: At your disposal.

Ben: We are at your disposal.

Ros: Would you gentlemen mind standing in the view of that man and me? I should not like him to spy me out. He is named Benvolio I have gathered, but I have not your introduction, my lord.

Mer: And you shall have... Benvolio, Is that your mother's, father's, uncle?

Ben: What are you talking about? My family wouldn't be caught dead at a Capulet...? (Mercutio hits Benvolio hard.) Oww!

Mer: Over there. (Hits him again.)

Ben: Why are you hitting me…? No you don't. I saw her here first.

Mer: You did not, you pushed me into her. I think obviously one could only assume you saw her not at all.

Ben: So, maybe I did it on purpose.

Mer: Why in the world would a man push another man into a lady at a party?

Ben: To say hello.

Mer: You really need to work on your approach man.

Tybalt a Capulet are seen talking quietly to the side at this time.

Ros: If you boys would like some privacy for your conversation I could go?

Ben: No, no my lady…

Mer: No we were just sorting some things out, complicated matters…completely unrelated…

Ben: Yes complicated and unrelated. You will owe me.

Mer: Indebted.

Ben: It has been my pleasure lady. Perhaps after, when my friend here has proven to be the great bore that we all know him to be, we shall talk again.

Ros: Perhaps, good Benvolio. And you?

Mer: I am Mercutio, fair lady.

Ros: Pleasure Mercutio.

Benvolio exits, Tybalt bursts out.

Tyb: Why, uncle, 'tis a shame!

Cap: Go to, Go to. You are a saucy boy Is't so indeed

This trick may chance to scathe you' I know what

You must contrary me! Marry. Tis time-

Well said my hearts!- You are a Princox: go,

Be quiet, or – More light, more light for shame!

I'll make you quiet- What, cheerly, my hearts!

Tybalt storms over.

Tyb: Come, I'm leaving.

Ros: I can hear that.

Tyb: Let's be gone.

Ros: I think I'll stay awhile.

Tyb: Do not push me woman, I've quite enough this night!

Mer: I think the lady has made her mind.

Tyb: You stay out of this business, tis none of your affair.

Mer: I owe this lady a debt, her affair now is my business.

Tyb: You listen now. Let's go. (Grabs Rosaline's arm roughly)

Mer: I think she's staying.

Tyb: Mercutio, what do think this a joke?

Mer: You are the only laughable thing I see.

Tyb: This woman is mine. Bought and paid for. When I say it's time to do something, she does it. (Rosaline winces as Tybalt gives her arm a twist.)

Mer: Not tonight. (Mercutio puts his hand on Tybalt's shoulder.)

Tyb: I will see you dead one day Mercutio.

Mer: Not tonight. Now maybe you should go, before your uncle has you escorted. (Mercutio about Tybalt both put hands on the hilt of swords.)

L.Cap: Gentlemen, for shame. Why are you not dancing? You men would not draw sword in this house would you?

Mer: Forgive me my Lady, I was only checking to see that it was still there. Verona streets can be most dangerous at night and I wouldn't want to be without it when I leave tonight.

L.Cap: I'm sure you would not. And such closeness to the Prince as yours can make a walk in the dark especially dangerous, I would think. Tell me, it would be most tragic if you were to be injured when you leave our party here tonight, can I arrange for you an escort to ensure safe passage?

Mer: Do not trouble yourself my Lady...

L.Cap: Tis no trouble Mercutio. It would dishonour this house greatly should anyone cause harm to our Prince's near-son when he leaves the safety of its walls.

Tyb: Auntie...

L.Cap: Quiet kitten!

Mer: I thank you for your most generous offer Lady Capulet. But I am not alone this evening and can assure you that no harm shall befall me, or that your house should suffer any dishonour by my part.

L.Cap: Merry, tis good to hear. Come Nephew, before you depart I should have word with you.

Tybalt stares at Mercutio and then at Rosaline a second, he then stalks off after Lady Capulet.

Mer: Nice lad. We go way back.

Ros: He has a temper like I've never seen.

Mer: Are you with him?

Ros: Not tonight.

Mer: Lady, may I ask why it is I am indebted this night to you? Why is it you do not wish to be seen by that Romeo?

Ros: I attended this ball this night with the thought that he was the last person I would be seeing. But it would seem Romeo the Montague would have a wish for death entering this place.

Mer: But Lady, you must be mistaken for I know this Romeo somewhat. And I would say he feels love much deeper than most, but I also know he only has eyes for one.

Ros: Three, by the way he is dancing with my cousin.

Mer: Tell me what offence did Romeo commit that would bar him from the company of such beautiful and pleasant maid as you?

Ros: I had met this Romeo some time ago and ever since I have received innumerable tokens from him. Poems that read like honey poured on a midden heap. He stands outside my chamber window some nights serenading me. It makes me desire the sound of a couple of tomcats in heat, to fight in a nearby alley as to drown out his song. I have had my servants put the run to him too many times I can't count. But he is convinced they do it because love between us is forbidden, and then he designs to try even harder for my affection. At any given point during day or night I'll turn, and out of the corner of my eye I can see him sighing, moaning; a lamenting figure watching me so piteously that I'm not sure if I should vomit or run for fear. It's really very unnerving. I'm sure I have been not much shy of the devil himself to him, meeting his proclamations of undying love with scorn and verbal blows that would castrate most men. But, like a great dullard he meets them with his jaw slack, eyes moony and I wonder sometimes if his hearing is stricken. Or maybe that he might not have a full compliment of chairs at his dining room table.

Mer: Well I'm sure a woman with your charms must be quite used to madmen following her around.

Ros: Well thank you Master Mercutio. I can see at least you are not without your own charm.

Mer: I have not however been totally forthright with you, I do know Romeo better than somewhat, in fact I am here tonight in his company.

Ros: Oh I am terribly sorry. I didn't realize such a man as he had friends.

Mer: It's true... Hold a second I think he is coming this way. Do not move.

Ros: Oh, don't let him see me.

At that Mercutio kisses Rosaline.

Mer: That was close mi' lady but I don't think he spied you.

Ros: That was not Romeo.

Mer: Really, you think? I was not fully certain but I though it best not to take chances.

Ros: You are fresh Master Mercutio.

Mer: I assure you my Lady, you enlisted me on this effort and I take that charge very seriously.

Ros: You do? Well I apologize Master Mercutio, I thought you an opportunist.

Mer: Quite alright but quickly we should make to the dance floor now.

Ros: The dance floor. You think being in plain view a wise strategy?

Mer: He'll never think to look there.

Ros: How logical. It would seem I am to be in the good hands of one who has done this before.

Mer: Countless times.

Ros: Lead on then my good man.

Mercutio and Rosaline make their way to dance.

L.Cap: Oh my dear sweet boy, you have so much to learn.

Tyb: Mine uncle, your husband has not only let the son of his greatest enemy eat from his table and drink from his cellar, but there the villain now takes the pleasure of your daughter's company too! It is a shame!

L.Cap: There is a time and place for everything my pet. Besides what harm can come from that Montague boy having a harmless dance with your cousin?

Tyb: I should cut his throat.

L.Cap: Maybe. But you will do no such thing this night my pet. Your uncle has expressly forbid it. And after that fiasco you created this morning that should be quite enough trouble for one day. No, we will bring down that boy and the whole of the house of Montague in a much more civilized manner. Peter!

Peter comes over and gives them both a drink. He is then waved off.

L.Cap: But tonight my pet nephew, everyone is to enjoy themselves and celebrate. Very soon your cousin will be married to Paris and Capulet will be joined with the house of Escalus. That is most worthy of a celebration. Just think pet, you and Mercutio will be kin!

Tyb: You do not think for a moment that a marriage will change anything?

L.Cap: Oh yes I do. I think there will be very significant changes after that marriage. Tell me, who do you think will rule Verona when Escalus dies?

Tyb: I will never bow and scrape before that worm should he sit on the throne of Verona.

L.Cap: I know my pet, trust me I'm counting on that. But Escalus is many things, a fool he is not. He would never entrust the rule of his beloved Verona to Mercutio. Although I can imagine the Montagues would be pressing very hard to see that done. No, I would think he has only two real choices to consider, the other one, the brother or our dear County Paris.

Tyb: Paris? On the throne? But he is so…

L.Cap: Weak?

Tyb: Yes.

L.Cap: But what choice does he have? A weak heir or one no one has ever seen?

Tyb: Anyone but Mercutio. Did you see how he interfered in my personal affairs with my future wife?

L.Cap: Well, if you did not make your personal affairs so public you would find you do not have such problems. But while we are on the topic of your upcoming nuptials, once that is done, Capulet will tie a good many allies new to it's house.

Tyb: But what difference does it all make? How does this possibly bring down the Montagues?

L.Cap: My dear sweet pet, it is such a good thing that you are as pretty as you are. But never fear Aunt Capulet will do all your thinking for you. The marriage of your cousin to Paris and yours to that girl, will bind so many houses of Verona to us, not to mention Escalus itself, that it will be as good as if the Capulet picked the heir to the throne. And we will be poised so that, within two generations, one of this house will be the very Prince of Verona. And Montague will find they have little or no influence left at all. And then that will be the time and the place for you to cut young Romeos throat.

Tyb: Is that what uncle has planned?

L.Cap: Your uncle? Oh no, not at all old Capulet can barely manage the affairs under his own roof, let alone plan the fate of Verona. No this is something that must be kept between us, you and me. You see my pet if anything, God forbid, should happen to my darling husband this house will need someone to lead it. Someone young, someone virile, like yourself to become its head. I would need your help guiding us to this end.

*Lady Capulet is inches away from Tybalt in almost a kiss. Tybalt
        motion as if to take her in his arms and she breaks away.*

L.Cap: Now, why don't you finish your drink and wait for
        me up in my chambers like a good kitten. I will
        attend to my guests and be up to meet you in a
        while.

Tyb: But what about Rosaline?

L.Cap: I'm sure she will manage without you. Now go.

*Tybalt exits as Lady Capulet fades back to join other guests. At the
        entrance Valentine is seen entering wearing a mask, his
        invitation in his hands. Capulet approaches, he is quite
        merry.*

Cap: Welcome, welcome my most excellent guest.
        (Reading invitation.) Signore Shylock of Venice so
        pleased to meet you! At last I am honored to have
        such a notable merchant in my home. (Val
        removes the mask) And a man of such young
        years, to be so successful.

Val: Well actually I'm...

Cap: Modest! I like that. I do hope perchance to speak a
        little business with you this night? I am hoping to
        expand my affairs and we could be very profitable
        together you and I.

Val: Yes I'm sure but the invitation...

Cap: I'd give a pound of my flesh for a drink of wine!
        Would you not as well? Will you join me Signore?
        I insist.

        Capulet signals Peter who brings wine.

Val: Oh why not?

Peter begins to pour.

Pete: My lord might I have a word with you if it would please you?

Cap: Go ahead Peter.

Pete: So please you my lord perhaps in private?

Cap: I am sure it is no matter that needs to be hidden from our Venetian guest.

Pete: It is a matter of the Montagues that needs be discussed. One is here, this night.

Cap: I know of this, Peter, this is not news. Did my nephew put you up to this?

Pete: Indeed lord Tybalt did mention the matter and bid me intervene.

Cap: I will tell you my mind as I told my rotten tempered nephew. Not a hair on the head of that boy will be harmed tonight. Do you understand Peter?

Pete: I do my lords bidding as always.

Cap: See that you do. This does embarrass your lord, for his guests to think he does not have control over his own house. Go to, and make it known to the house that any harm on that Montague boy will be three fold to the one that inflicted it. Does your master make himself clear Peter?

Pete: He does, and I will my lord.

Cap: A good man Peter, but I afraid it is a tenuous grip at times controlling such hatred of our enemies.

Val: Tolerance of ones enemies is difficult at the best of times.

Cap: I'm glad you understand. The truth is, as far as Montagues go, I hate the very ground they walk upon, but I can't hold any malice to this young man only to his hated name.

Enter Paris.

Cap: Ah County Paris! Welcome! This fine Count is soon to be my son, my Juliet's husband... (Peter re-enters and motions Cap) Gentlemen please, will you excuse me a moment whilst I tend to the needs of some guests.

Par: Valentine I'm surprised to see you here.

Val: Not half as I to hear your news.

Par: T'was just arranged.

Val: I'm happy for you... both.

Par: We need to talk.

Val: Is this not talk Paris?

Par: Valentine...

Val: Years ago.

Par: You're to be a priest.

Val: And you a husband. Truth is I think it has all worked out for the best. I'm sure you feel the same? I mean you are about to marry a fine young lady, so I'm sure you have had no trouble reconciling your past.

Par: Valentine you need to understand some things don't change.

Val: That is too true Paris. If you will excuse me I should be off to join the party.

Paris tries to stop Valentine by gently putting his hand on his chest, but Valentine breaks away. During this time Benvolio is seen speaking with Romeo.

Ben: Away be gone; the sport is at the best.

Rom: Ay so I fear; the more is my unrest.

Mercutio and Rosaline appear. Val puts on his visor.

Mer: You danced me out.

Ros: It appears your friends are leaving.

Mer: Leaving? But alas I too must go then, if it were not some great need for me to accompany them then I would... I would to like to stay the night here in your divine company.

Ros: You are off to run with your boys?

Mer: I would only to see them home safely.

Ros: Well then Mercutio, I guess if there is no more need to have your intervention, I release you of your charge then.

Mer: I humbly and most regrettably take my leave of you my lady. Can I call on you?

Ros: Depends, my cousin may now need your services.

Mer: Only one per family I'm afraid.

Ros: Well in that case then we shall see.

Mer: (Starts to follow then turns.) Lady?

Ros: Yes.

Mer: I will be more able to call sometime if I had the pleasure of my lady's name.

Ros: It's Rosaline.

Mer: You are fair Rosaline.

Starts to follow again turns comes back and kisses her on the cheek.
Mercutio joins at the door.

Cap: Nay, Gentlemen, prepare not to be gone;

We have a trifling foolish banquet towards...

Re-enter Peter taking Capulet to the side.

Pete: My lord I did, as you would have me instructed but to no avail. My lord Tybalt is drunk and enraged and he intends to kill Romeo as he leaves the house this very night.

Cap: Is it e'en so? Why, then, I thank you all:

I thank you, honest gentlemen; good night.

More torches here; come on! then let's to bed.

(To Valentine.) Ah, sirrah, by my fay it waxes late:

I'll to my rest.

Exit Capulet and Peter in a hurry. Romeo, Mercutio and Ben exit.
Juliet and the nurse are seen talking quietly then leaving.
Only Valentine and Rosaline are left.

Val: You were a cat I see this night?

Ros: What? Oh yes, you were a...?

Val: A frog... I think? The party's at an end then?

Ros: Mostly. There are still a few revelers in the courtyard.

Val: Ah. I should be going too as well, I have things to do.

Ros: What sort of things would need doing at this late hour?

Val: The beauty with books is that they can be read at any hour day or night. So long as you have a candle that is to say.

Ros: It does help in the dark. And what books would you be reading my lord?

Val: A few. But mostly Summa Perfectionis for the time.

Ros: Geber. Where on earth did you get a copy of that book? That must be 11th century.

Val: 10th actually. My library is quite extensive, but I had a devil of a time getting that copy. You are familiar with alchemy?

Ros: I find the theories fascinating. All matter in the universe having a perfectionus state and once brought to that place it becomes almost spiritual.

Val: Yes. Like if matter is transformed to that state that it very likely it would become, as a candle flame radiating heat and light.

Ros: So then you feel fire is in its perfectionus state?

Val: No not quite perfect but close. If fire were perfect it would need no fuel and it would leave no ash and burn indefinitely.

Ros: You think this could be done?

Val: Maybe? And not just with fire but wood, stone even flesh maybe.

Ros: If you are correct then that wall and that door and maybe even you and me, we are really all just made up of imperfect light?

Val: Of course. Perfect light that was made into imperfect matter. I'm Valentine. You are?

Ros: Rosaline.

Val: You don't say? Would you mind if a fellow book appreciator walked you home lady Rosaline?

Ros: It would be a pleasure.

They exit.

ACT THREE

Lights up on Valentines study.

Val: Has there ever been someone in your life… a girl I mean, before you became…?

Law: Celibate?

Val: Yes.

Law: It's good to remember my son that "all have sinned and fell short of the glory of God." But once forgiven, you are forever absolved of that transgression. I did find love as a young man before I chose a celibate life. But once lost, that perfect love, I knew it could not happen twice in a lifetime.

Val: It's foolish but there was a part of me that thought, if I were on this path, that I would be tempted by flesh no more.

Law: Do you speak of love, my son?

Val: No. It could never be. I've decided to put it out of my mind. Love is a very strange sort of animal. It is best to be celibate and be done with it.

Law: I see. Valentine, be sure that love is beautiful and it is a shame one can't be a priest and husband, but alas that is the way of things. A life of celibacy is probably the most difficult oath a man could ever swear. It's the mark of devotion to God, him before all other worldly pleasures even the greatest of which. But do know this, my son, it is not something every man can do and there is no shame in that. I do hope this does not mean you are having second thoughts?

Val: No, Father. Escalus has said that you and he were speaking

Law: About what?

Val :You and he agreed I would enter as a Franciscan Brotherhood over the Jesuit order.

Law: The Prince and I did speak and we both agreed that it would be best on many levels.

Val: Well the Jesuits on many levels in terms of my education, I feel is best. I must say, I can't help but be a little angry.

Law: I know the Franciscan Brotherhood is not as new and up to date as the Jesuits but, if you join their order, there is no hope of you ever returning to Verona. Your cousin thought Mercutio would need you in the future.

Val : He has told you about his plans for him?

Law: He laid it out.

Val: That's all well, but should it not be my decision?

Law: It is most complicated Valentine. Please forgive me, I only want what's best for all.

Val: I'm sure. So father, what is your news that brought you so hastily to my cell on this hot morning?

Law: I have the most wondrous news to share with you and you must promise to keep it most secret.

Val: I shall.

Law: A physician, this morning, awoke me. He was seeking herbs for some illness across town. At any rate as I was in my grow house, who then but Romeo stops by. It would seem the landscape of this one's love has once again shifted. Romeo imparted to me that gone is the old love to be replaced now with none other than the daughter of his father's enemy. Romeo loves Juliet.

Val: But Friar this is most dreadful!

Law: And at first that was my very thought. The boy falls in love more often than we change clothes. But this time she loves him as well.

Val: You have this for sure Juliet loves him back?

Law: Romeo said they did exchange vows.

Val: But Juliet is to marry County Paris?

Law: It's a marriage of houses nothing more. But there is no love there.

Val: Why say you that?

Law: Son when you have seen as many married as I, you start to gain the ability to cipher such things.

Val: Does Juliet love Paris?

Law: Romeo would tell us no.

Val: Is it right then? To unite such a pair in holy sacrament without love?

Law: If that is the wishes of those involved, as members of the Church we are not to deny this. Love is theirs to find, not ours to judge.

Val: I can't imagine a worse union.

Law: There is no force on earth more powerful and more able to change than love. I had forgot that all these years surrounded by hate but this boy and girl, children of enemies reminded me that all black hate can be burned away with pure love.

Val: I don't agree father. What if Romeo falls out of love again?

Law: Son, there are forces at work around him, forces that direct him towards something. I don't know what? But I can feel it. And sure that in the ages to come the names of Romeo and Juliet will be synonymous with Love.

Val: Maybe so but you are never going to get Capulet and Montague to accept this.

Law: I'm sure this will all work out for the best with the happiest of endings.

Val: That is, if parents agree.

Law: Even without blessing.

Val: Father you cannot be thinking to marry them without parental blessing?

Law: You said it yourself. What's better what the parents want? Or would it be better to join Juliet with Paris without love?

Val: No… Not at all but…

Law: Have faith in love. The arrangement with Paris is more about business than the business of love.

Val: This is madness! The other day the houses rioted over mere words and now you will unit them as family, without their consent?

Law: I am not a madman! But there are mad lengths men must go to for peace. I had hoped you to share my faith. I had hoped you would understand that peace is the most important. And peace can be only found through love.

Val: This will only bring war.

Law: I say it will bring love. It is the only way.

Val: Romeo and Juliet will only end in tragedy.

Law: Your lack of faith disappoints me.

There is a knock at the door

Ser: Lady to see you here my lord.

Val: Ah...

Law: I'd best be going. Please remember your promise.

Val: It will be so, as I promised. But please father think this through, please reconsider.

Law: The Lord will guide us as always my son.

Lawrence leaves as Rosaline enters.

Ros: Good-morrow.

Rosaline goes to meet him.

Val: God ye good-morrow my Lady.

Awkward pause for a moment where Rosaline stands very close.

Ros: Your man let me in, I hope you don't mind.

Val: Not at all.

Ros: I remembered last night you said there were some volumes I might borrow.

Val: Indeed.

Ros: I was at the market and I saw these. I thought you might like them.

She gives Valentine flowers. Valentine breaks away.

Val: Flowers, that's... thank you they are beautiful. Can I get you anything? Wine?

Ros: Please.

Val: You'll have to forgive me I'm not accustomed to entertaining ladies just men visitors mostly, not that I wouldn't mind having more women... I mean, women to entertain… That is, you are a woman and the place is a real mess and rambling off the tongue aren't I?

Ros: A bit.

Val: I'm sorry.

Ros: Not at all I'm charmed. The matter is, I needed to see you… I mean speak with you myself.

Val: No please if I may? I also wanted to speak with you. First thing I would like to make it clear that there is nothing in this world I would like more than us to spend time together. I find our conversations very interesting… But…

Ros: But?

Val: You need to understand my clear intentions. I should have mentioned to you that I'm about to enter the priesthood.

Ros: Oh…. Well, there goes that proposal I had all ready go this morning… I am kidding you Valentine.

Val: I just didn't want there to be any misunderstandings between us, you and I. For a number of years now I have been preparing for this and now the Prince and the Friar and a good many others are expecting me to go this way.

Ros: And you Valentine, how do you feel about this decision?

Val: What do you mean?

Ros: It's just that you mentioned that the Friar, the Prince and others are expecting this. How do you feel about it?

Val : I don't question it. It's the best way to get an education. I should like being in the priesthood I think. It has always felt right, felt like the best place for me.

Ros: That's good I should like to have a priest for a friend to hear my all my darkest, nocturnal confessions. Valentine do you think me pretty?

Val: Sure?

Ros: Sure…?

Val : Of course you are pretty… I'm sorry I've hurt your feelings.

Ros: No don't be sorry I should not have put you in that spot.

Val: Rosaline, I am sorry I just don't <u>feel</u> that way.

Ros: I should let you get back to work.

Val : I do like your company I find it a most pleasant distraction.

Ros: Distraction? How sweet.

Valentine stops her at the door.

Val : Rosaline please don't go. Not like this.

Rosaline hesitates and then sits.

Val: You are very beautiful and any man would be the luckiest fool I could know to have your heart, but believe me when I say, I am a fool but I'm not he.

Ros: Please understand me Master Valentine; I never throw myself like that. I just found you to be interesting and I thought you might find me that way as well.

Val: I find you fascinating.. And I would love us to be nothing less than the best of friends. Why don't we start over?

Ros: Good idea I'd love another chance to become an even bigger fool.

Val: Here, stand up. You make like to enter again.

She moves to exit and stands.

Val: Oh hullo!

Ros: Your man let me in. I brought you flowers in a strictly platonic manner of friendship.

Val: In the same manner I accept this generous gift and am surprised and elated to receive your company.

Ros: I know such a busy man, as yourself, needs to have a pleasant distraction from time to time. I would like to distract you.

Val: And a woman as pretty as you, needs never to throw herself at an otherwise distracted man.

They laugh. Rosaline starts to cough slightly.

Ros: You do laugh Signore Valentine.

Val: From time to time.

Ros: I'm glad we started over. A most excellent idea.

Val: Friends?

Ros: Friends. (Goes to sculpture.) This is nice is it yours?

Val: Yes.

Ros You are an artist as well as an academic?

Val: Artist? Not at all.

Ros: Why? Wouldn't you say that it's lovely?

Val: The proportions are incorrect. It cannot be divided by Phi.

Ros: What is that?

Val: Phi, it's Greek for 1.618, the perfect number. The masters use it to get the proportions in their work perfect. If you divide the distance from you hip to the floor by the distance of your knee to the floor it will be 1.618. The same goes with shoulders and elbows, facial proportions, fingers and toes, etcetera.

Ros: There is so much more freedom in raw creation. So much more beauty in a form that hasn't been added, subtracted, multiplied and divided to death.

Val: Well maybe when I'm finished it could be a gift?

Ros: I'd like that. Only thing is I'm leaving Verona.

Val: You are? Where are you going?

Ros: I'm going to Venice.

Val: For how long?

Ros: I'm not coming back.

Val: You moving with family?

Ros: More like from family. I'm planning to disappear from Verona and my betrothed.

Val: Are you betrothed?

Ros: I have been betrothed since I was a child. I am to marry Tybalt the Capulet.

Val: Tybalt. Mercutio has no love there.

Ros: Mercutio?

Val: My brother.

Ros: We met at Capulet's last night. Good dancer, a perfect gentleman.

Val: Mercutio?

Ros: I might have guessed there was something more than met the eye there when he leapt to defend me from Tybalt. Truth is, I'm afraid I really have not spent a great deal of time with my future husband. Can I be candid Valentine?

Val: Of course.

Ros: Not only am I not in love with Tybalt, but as a matter of fact I don't think I even like him. He is a mean man. And frankly he scares me. My house is not a very well off but our name and connections are of the very best in Verona. My father is not a prosperous man and when I was a child the families made arrangements.

Val: What will you do?

Ros: If I stay here there is nothing I can do, Tybalt will be my husband.

Val: Have you told your father this marriage is not to your liking?

Ros: I did some time ago and I could not leave the house for several weeks because of the bruising.

Val: Your Father beat you?

Ros: At least when Tybalt hits me he won't mark my face. He says if the bruising can be seen by others they see weakness and think he hasn't control in his own house.

Val: Could you not marry someone else? A noble from a different house, maybe an even better house?

Ros: Do you have someone in mind...? It would not change anything. Shortly after the arrangement was made my father borrowed so heavily from his future son in-law that he has no means of ever paying the debt back. Tybalt becoming family is all that keeps father from becoming ruined. But who knows, maybe there is still a chance that Tybalt will go ahead and marry his Aunt Capulet, for there is his true love I'm sure of it.

Val: Surely you jest.

Ros: Failing that, I will be married soon. But not until his cousin Juliet is united with the County Paris. Capulet feels this will solidify him with the Prince. Is he not your cousin Valentine?

Val: Paris is the son of Escalus' mother's brother, he is not my blood.

Ros: Marriages all around eh? But none for you I should say padre? Did you not ever think about marriage?

Val: Not really.

Ros: What, you don't envy the happiness I will be having in my nuptials? Tell me what she would be like?

Val: I would not be a good husband.

Ros: Nonsense I'm sure you would make a perfect husband. Have you ever been in love?

Val: Yes.

Ros: Was she beautiful? ...Oh come on Valentine we were just starting to have good conversation. I know so little about you. Tell me how did your parents died then?

Val: Lost at sea.

Ros: That's terrible. How old were you?

Val: Mercutio and I were very young, I can remember them a little but he says he has no memories of them.

Ros: What were they like?

Val: Mother had a kind face and father I remembered to be very serious.

Ros: They sound the composite of you. I'm sure they would be very proud of the man you became. There is rumour you lock yourself up here for months at a time is that true?

Val: I have work to do.

Ros: What are you doing up here that is so important to be alone?

Val: Pursuing perfection I guess you'd say.

Ros: You call that perfection? Since when has isolation and loneliness become perfect?

Val: How would you know if I was lonely or not?

Ros: It doesn't take a genius to see you are miserable Valentine.

Val: I don't see why everyone around me thinks that the natural state of the human condition is to be happy. Happiness is not a right that is due to us. Happiness is not even a realistic expectation for life. Mankind had the chance to be happy when we were perfect, and we ruined that.

Ros: So how you are going to be our salvation here alone in your study?

Val: I can try to change it.

Ros: You are unhappy so you devote your life to finding a cure by cutting yourself off from anything that could make you happy? I think you might be on to something there.

Val: You know what I'm looking forward to the most about the monastery? I'm looking forward to the isolation. Nobody needing anything from me. I will not have to spy for them or go to meaningless parties and nobody will care if I disappear for months or even years. I don't want to care about Mercutio and what he's doing, I don't want to care about the Prince and Verona. I never asked to be the one to make all those problems better.

Ros: The world is not your experiment Valentine. You are not some impartial observer. You are part of the experiment and part of it all. You can't watch from some distant tower and not effect the outcome.

Val: If I take myself out of the world then the world will go on just fine. And I can decide what I like and what I do not.

Ros: What about those who love you?

Val: That is the problem. Love was never intended to be a part of the world. It is a by-product of human attachment it has no rightful place in this universe. We create it! It is not divine, heaven just looks down at us and watches in sad impartiality as we commit horrible acts in the name of it. Love of country, love of a woman or the love of our own ideals and it weeps at our moral justifications for our atrocities.

Ros: That is not true, what about acts performed for no other reasons but pure love?

Val: There is no such thing, just the impurity and selfishness. Those acts are done for no other reason than to make one feel better against all the wrongs they have already heaped on this world.

Ros: That is so sad.

Rosaline begins to cough uncontrollably. She is having difficulty breathing.

Val: Are you alright? Here have a drink. (She faints and Valentine catches her. He moves her to the chair.) Stay here a moment. (Valentine pulls a cord to ring for help. In moments a servant enters.) Help me with this lady she seems to be over come.

Ser: Yes my lord.

Lights down as Valentine and the servant are moving Rosaline.

Lights.

Valentine's study later that morning. Mercutio sits in a chair with a slight possible hangover, he is holding Valentine's mask. Valentine enters.

Mer: Where have you been?

Val: I had to go out very early this morning.

Mer: You forgot your disguise? (Holds up mask.)

Val: What? Oh that? One of the servants found it in the palace they thought it have been yours from last night.

Mer: No, not mine.

Val: You are up early. How was last night?

Mer: Up late actually. And most excellent thank you. You shouldn't have missed it.

Val: I trust our young Romeo is alive and well?

Mer: To be perfectly honest I am not sure, he gave us the slip. I do know he made it out of the Capulet house intact but we lost him shortly after. But I'm sure the watch will find him if he's dead.

Val: I'm sure he is at home. That was awfully stupid of the lads to go there.

Mer: It was fine, Capulet did not even suspect.

Val: Maybe not, but what if he had? What if the whole of his house came out to get Romeo? What would you have done?

Mer: I would have been loyal to my friend.

Val: About loyalty, Mercutio what about your Prince, our cousin-father? Would you not owe him some sense of loyalty?

Mer: So now Escalus is to say who my friends shall be?

Val: No but you talk of loyalty and you impede the peace process with your actions, a peace which is the very mandate of the head of your house. You do more than disloyalty to your friends when you do this treason to your own house.

Mer: Treason. Well said Valentine. Tell me, did Escalus write that for you? Because you are sounding an awful lot like him just there.

Val: Mercutio please...

Mer: Is this you brother? Or is it the Prince speaking?

Val: Mercutio this is very serious.

Mer: So am I. You have never lied to me, brother. We
       have always been honest with each other. But tell
       me, did Escalus recruit you for his little mission to
       control Mercutio? Tell me the truth I have very
       few whom I can trust.

Val: I am not on a mission from Escalus.

Mer: What a relief. Forgive me, but it's just that I've
       heard quite enough about this from our Prince
       lately. I'm sick to death of the subject. Let me tell
       you what I've already told Escalus. I have no
       control over who my friends might be, nor who
       my family is or who my enemies are. I would hate
       Tybalt were he a Montague and I would be friend
       to Romeo were he a Capulet. This feud has
       nothing to do with me. I can neither fight it nor
       fix it. Now if you are done playing at lectures?

Val: Fine. So what keeps you from your bed brother?

Mer: That which I found last night. And am not sure I
       can keep.

Val: A purse full of gold?

Mer: Better, worth more. I think I am in love brother.

Val: You? Eros stole your heart over another serving
       girl?

Mer: Wrong and wrong. You think you know me so
       well brother. It is not a serving girl, it is a Lady, a
       Lady! And it was not Eros it was his son the one
       who makes lovers speak in couplets.

Val: Who is she?

Mer: Ay, that's the rub that is what robs me of sleep.
       This excellent woman; the queen of my heart
       belongs in another's heart. Or so that is how he
       would have it.

Val: She is his love?

Mer: Not precisely. She is but loved.

Val: Does this lady return your favor?

Mer: Time will tell.

Val :   This Lady was at Capulet's last night?

Mer: No she was at the Sister's of Mercy cloister. Of course she was at Capulet's where else did you think I went last night? Keep up. You should have come Valentine.

Val: I'm sure.

Mer: At the mask she wore a cat face.

Val :   Cat face.

Mer: I've always liked cats. You know there are two kinds of people in the world those who are dog people and those who are cat people I think I'm the latter. You are definitely a dog person Valentine. Well I'm spent. I'll to my truckle bed, good night brother.

Val: Good morrow.

Servant enters.

Ser: My lord, we have made arrangements for the Lady Rosaline to be taken home.

Val: Thank you. That is all...

Mer: What's this?

Servant exits.

Mer: What is he talking about... Rosaline?

Val: Mercutio...

Mer: You bastard. That explains the mask.

Val: Mercutio I can explain...

Mer: You couldn't stand it could you? As soon as I had a little happiness you just had to see if you could destroy it.

Val: It's not like that, Rosaline and I are just friends.

Mer: Just friends? Is that how you treat your friends?

Val: Would you just listen for once?

Mer: How long have you two been doing this?

Val: This? There is no "this". We just met.

Mer: When? This morning? Sometime in the night did she come through your window? When?

Val: Last night. We met at the Capulet feast.

Mer: You came after all? I didn't see you there. Why didn't say hello brother? Or did you just quietly want to watch your brother's back to spy out where the knife would go?

Val: Somebody's got to keep you out of trouble.

Mer: Who designated you? Let me guess Escalus?

Val: Escalus asked me to go.

Mer: So now you are a liar Valentine. You have been conspiring with the Prince.

Val: There is no conspiracy. Mercutio.

Mer: You spy for the prince at night and steal kisses in the private during the day. That seems truth enough for my eyes. Not a good start to life in the clergy brother.

Val: When are you going to grow up Mercutio? When are you going to stop being a self absorbed, adolescent child and grow up?

Mer: At least I am grown enough not to take my brothers woman!

Val: She was not your woman. You danced with her one night, that's all!

Mer: And then my brother Pope Pious decided to remove his cloth!

Val: I'm through with you. Get out Mercutio!

Mer: What's the matter brother? Touch a nerve, a little crisis of faith?

Valentine grabs Mercutio and pushes him towards the door.

Val: If you do not leave I will make you!

Mer: You don't tell me what to do.

Val: That's right! That's what I heard about your life as a soldier. It's hard to follow orders when "nobody tells you what to do."

Mer: You have no idea what you're talking about Valentine.

Val: What's the matter now? Touch a nerve?

Mercutio and Valentines begin to fight. The fight goes for some time and ends with Valentine on the desk with Mercutio over him holding a knife to his throat. Mercutio screams and then drops the knife.

Mer: It's only because you are my brother I don't cut your throat just now. While you sat here in the comfort of this palace studying your old books I was sent to bleed and die somewhere on the Spanish border.

Val: Our Cousin gave you a good opportunity and like all good things you squandered it.

Mercutio let's Valentine up.

Mer: Do you know where our militia gets its fine officers? Our brass is made up of the younger son's of noblemen who haven't any lands or titles to inherit. One such officer in the service of the Prince was my commanding officer, Tybalt the Capulet. We were tasked to attack on a rat's nest of Spaniards we more than out numbered. I was ordered to have my men take point, on Tybalt's command. Unfortunately for us, at the last moment our dear Tybalt called off the rear of the attack. This was too bad for us though as we were already engaged. We were like lambs to the slaughter. I lost everyone except one man.

Val: What did Escalus do?

Mer: Nothing. You know, if I had not been the Prince's kinsman in the first place, they would have stuck me in the lower ranks where I belonged.

Val: Does he know these details?

Mer: Of coarse he does.

Val: Is there someone who can tell your side?

Mer: Don't be a fool, Valentine, there is nobody who cares. What's done is done. Verona politics protect Tybalt from being held up to any real justice. Fear of civil war in Verona protects him. So now that I have educated you on this subject how would you like to join me in a drink and a toast to the Prince's soldiers? No? Well I'll have one. (He pours drink)

The door opens Escalus enters.

Mer: Well the devil himself. Cousin, you're just in time for a toast.

Val: Mercutio!

Mer: Stand down brother. What better reason to drink than the health of your sovereign, I always say. To Escalus the Prince of Verona, Defender of Italia's borders etcetera, etcetera. May he live long to keep Verona safe and peaceful. And like our savior who rode his ass to Jerusalem to bring peace. Here too may our prince, like the ass, bring peace, to Verona.

Esc: You mock me Mercutio?

Val: Forgive him your highness he's not himself.

Mer: On the contrary brother I am quite myself as a matter of fact I'm starting to understand things a lot more and see it all quite clearly. Did you come to consult with your little Judas spy, your highness? To see what he has been able to glean through his intrigues?

Esc: Mercutio mind your tone.

Mer: Or what? Will you lock me in prison? I won't be able embarrass you with my friends and bring shame to your house that way? Or better yet why don't you send me to war… well that didn't work out so well the first time.

Esc: Whatever it takes, Mercutio, to get you in line.

Mer: It's a shame you weren't here just a second ago, I was telling Valentine about our efforts on the borders and how things are going. He found it quite enlightening

69

Esc: You disobeyed your orders.

Mer: Lies! He never gave me that order! That court was put together by you with the instruction to find Tybalt innocent on all accounts at any cost!

Esc: If Tybalt were hanged Verona would fall into chaos!

Mer: So I took all the shame and dishonor!

Esc: Maybe it's time you deal with those demons and move on.

Mer: Is that your advice? Well thank you your highness, that's just what I needed. A royal command. Tonight, for a change, I shall not awake screaming and soaked with sweat after seeing the bloody faces of my comrades lost that day. And when next I meet the other survivor of that high point in my life, I'll say "Do not scowl at me, my legless friend, for the Prince has commanded your pardon."

Esc: An officer will lose soldiers.

Mer: But I am no officer, I will never be an officer! Their lives should not have been my responsibility I never wanted it!

Esc: A man takes on responsibility.

Mer: Responsibility! You sent me away hoping I would die! You would finally be rid of your Cousin's troublesome son! But I returned an even bigger disgrace.

Esc: My responsibility to you and your father I do not take lightly, I mourn his loss every day. My hopes for you Mercutio is that you would become the man he was. But I have been able to teach you nothing! I welcomed you back after that failure and you spat in my face!

Mer: My failure? Welcomed me back? Can you hear this brother? If I remember right you sat all through the inquiry, arms folded and not once opened your mouth to my defense. As Tybalt heaped lie after lie about his orders to disengage. Even with a mountain of evidence to the contrary you decided that you would rather see me take a fall, all for the sake of your so-called "peace"!

Esc: If I had not ruled as I did Tybalt would have been executed!

Mer: Let him! It would have been justice! And it would have saved me the trouble!

Esc: Justice or no the Capulets would revolt.

Mer: Let them! Let them destroy Verona and burn this palace to the ground!

Esc: You would have them do that wouldn't you Mercutio? Bringing their enemies into their own homes.

Mer: Romeo and Benvolio went of their own accord. I did not bring anyone!

Esc: It was your doing!

Mer: No it was not!

Val: My lord I think he's right, Romeo and Benvolio acted on their own.

Mer: Listen to your skirt chasing toady, Escalus. He would know, if you don't believe me.

Esc: It would do you well to seek your Prince's favor as much as half your brother Mercutio.

Mer: I have no loyalty to you. (He spits.)

Esc: Because of who your father was I will forgive you this treason, but just once boy! Know this, better men have seen the headsman for lesser words. You leave me no choice boy. You favour truth so much, here is a truth. Your brother is to leave for the monastery his fate is in motion. I have no other worthy heirs so that leaves only you. I say you will be Prince after me one day, and I will not let that happen till I think you can do it and well it be done. For this reason, you will change your ways and bend to my will. From now henceforth my command to you is, no more contact with any Montague unless on state business. You risk all plans to keep peace and it will stop now. Do you understand?

Mer: Romeo is my friend. You think I'll obey you?

Esc: If loyalty to me will not do it then loyalty to your friend will be enough to carry it through. For Romeo is the cause of this feud. Romeo is the son of his father's enemy! The bastard product of an adulterous union of Capulet and Montague.

Mer: You lie!

Esc: Capulet hates Montague for raising his own son to hate his very father. And Montague teaches him that hate to spite his enemy Capulet!

Mer: You lie!

Esc: That's the truth!

Val: Oh my god...

Mer: Romeo a Capulet?

Esc: It is so.

Mer: Romeo must know of this.

Esc: He is a bastard. If this secret ever gets out it will destroy him. Think Mercutio, if you revealed this to spite me you would only bring ruin to his life and accomplish nothing but disloyalty to your friend.

Mer: Romeo should know his real father.

Esc: To what end? Which is his real father the one that sired him as a bastard or the one he grew up calling father legitimate? Would it be beneficial for your friend to know such a painful truth? As a ruler, you will have secrets, secrets that no one can know. When you take the throne the burden of Verona's best-kept secrets will affect every aspect of your rule, decisions and associations. Maybe now you can understand why I've had to make the decisions I have made. I'm not expecting you to forgive me, only to understand.

Mer: Well you have it all figured out cousin. You are right. I will take this to my grave and act accordingly. But, know this, I ask not for your throne or Verona's secrets. I will die before being your heir.

Servant enters carrying Rosaline her dress is torn. She has been badly hurt and can't walk.

Val: Rosaline! Fetch a physician!

Ser: At once.

Valentine and Mercutio go to Rosaline.

Val : What happened?

Ros: Forgive me Valentine, I had nowhere else to go. When I was returned home this morning I found Tybalt in a rage.

Val: He did this to you?

Rosaline weeps. Mercutio goes to the door.

Val: Mercutio wait!

Mer: No worries Val. I just need some air.

Mercutio exits.

Val: Cousin...?

Esc: I'm on it. And I'll see if I can't hurry the doctor.

Escalus exits.

Val: It's all fine... everything is alright. Where are you hurt?

Ros: He kicked me. Over and over but see, he never touched my face. I'm scared Valentine.

Val: It's going to be alright, the doctor will be here soon.

Ros: I've been thinking about what you said Valentine, about kindness. Maybe you are right; maybe we only are kind because charitable acts make us feel better. Selfish or no though, I think that it is better to live in that world than it is to live in this one. You can't become something you are not just to escape how your own feelings, that's no reason to be priest.

Val: Just lay still...

Ros: Leave Verona Valentine, go and be happy.

Val: Rosaline, I can't just run away, there are matters and responsibilities that I have to attend to.

Ros: The matters and responsibilities that bind you to this city are not yours. You can't fix them. Let the others have them. There is sadness about you and I think that comes from being the only one that ever meets expectations, while having yours continually disappointed over and over. So you stay cooped up in this study with your books and experiments waiting for a perfect life to come to your door. But let's face it, that is not going to happen. Here the only thing coming through that door is more pain, more news that is going to make you even unhappier. It is sometimes selfish to be kind but sometimes you have to be kind to yourself.

Val: I can never have what makes me happy.

Ros: Only because you will not.

Val: No it was taken from me. It was the loss of my lover that has left me so unhappy. You said you wanted to know something about me, well here's the truth. I was forbidden to be with him and he was taken away from me. I fell in love with him three summers ago. We would steal away together to a secret place known only to the two of us. He was the first I ever felt that kind of love for, and I know too for the time he loved me as well. But alas we were found out. Our love was rewarded with shame and humiliation. We were driven apart with threats, ridicule and denigration, I will never love again. And now, he is to be married to Capulet's daughter.

Ros: Paris?

Val: He is … was my love.

Ros: Oh my poor sweet Valentine.

Val: This is why I must go into the service of God and finish my work.

Ros: How is that?

Val: To be forgiven. How can God forgive what I can never confess? There can be no forgiveness without confession. My only hope is that with a life to the service of God and work that would rediscover forgotten perfection, maybe heaven wouldn't refuse me if I could be perfect?

Ros: Valentine you already are. I have just heard your confession and no God I could ever imagine would think any less. Be free my friend, and thank you, thank you for your friendship. I was so afraid I might have died alone.

Val: No, no don't talk like that. Don't you do it Rosa, don't you leave me!

Ros: I have found my wings my heart, now you find yours...

Val: No, no, no... Rosaline, please the doctor is coming. Wake up, please...

Valentine sits holding Rosaline for a time. Servant enters.

Ser: My lord... The lady?

Val: Gone.

Ser: The surgeon can't be reached, there has been an outbreak of plague in the city.

Val: It is too late.

Lights up. A Street.

Mer: Tybalt you rat-catcher, will you walk?

Tyb: What wouldst thou have with me?

Mer: Good King of Cats, nothing but one of

your nine that I mean to make bold withal and,

as you shall use me hereafter, dry-beat the rest of the

eight. Will you pluck your sword out of his pilcher
by his ears? Make haste, lest mine be about your
ears ere it be out.

Tyb: I am for you.

Rom: Gentle Mercutio, put thy rapier up.

Mer: Come sir your passado.

They Fight.

Rom: Draw, Benvolio: beat down their weapons.
Gentlemen, for shame forbear this outrage.
Tybalt, Mercutio, the prince expressly hath
Forbid this bandying in Verona streets.
Hold, Tybalt! good Mercutio!

Tybalt under Romeo's arm thrusts Mercutio in and flies.

Mer: I am hurt
A plague o' both your houses! I am sped.
Is he gone and hath nothing?

Ben: What are you hurt?

Mer: Ay, ay, a scratch, a scratch; marry 'tis enough.
Where is my page? Go, villain, fetch a surgeon.

Rom: Courage, man; the hurt cannot be much.

Mer: No, 'tis not so deep as a well, nor so wide
As a church door, but 'tis enough, 'twill serve. Ask
For me tomorrow and you shall find me a grave
man. I am peppered, I warrant, for this world. A
plague o' both your houses! Zounds! A dog, a rat,

a mouse, a cat, to scratch a man to death! A braggart,

a rogue, a villain, that fights by the book of

arithmetic! Why the devil came you between us?

I was hurt under your arm.

Rom: I thought all for the best.

Mer: Help into some house, Benvolio,

Or I shall faint. A plague o' both your houses!

They have made worms' meat of me. I have it,

And soundly too. Your houses!

Benvolio helps Mercutio away. Lights.

Lights up on Valentines study, Val is packing his things in a bag. Shortly Benvolio and wounded Mercutio enter.

Val: Jesus, father in heaven! What has happened?

Ben: It was Tybalt. He's bleeding! I didn't know what to do?

Valentine uses his arm to clear the stuff off and on to the floor. Benvolio helps Mercutio on to the desk. Benvolio exits.

Val: Get him on the desk I'll do what I can, go as fast as you can and get a surgeon Benvolio.

Val: It's okay Mercutio Benvolio will get a surgeon.

Mer: Don't bother. I don't want one.

Val: Mercutio let me help you!

Mer: I am going to die.

Val: You can't you are...

Mer: Leave me be! I've enough of this world. My only regret being I didn't take Tybalt with me.

Val: Don't talk like that! Where is that surgeon!

Mer: Leave me! Let me die! Let Romeo, Escalus, you and your damn surgeon go to hell I will be there to meet!

Val: I'm sorry Mercutio... I'm so sorry... please, please not you too brother.

Mer: You were right to go in seclusion here. To stay away from people, people bring pain and every minute you spend with them is another minute we only cause each other hurt. I've always hated you a little bit, brother, I think for you knowing our parents and not I. But now I go to them before you.

Val :   You can't leave me brother.

Mer: Yes I can...

Val: Will you forgive me?

Mer: You can't hurt me now and I can't hurt you, there is nothing to forgive. You will make an excellent priest... oh father...!

Mercutio dies. Val weeps. Lights down.

Lights up on study Valentine is finishing a letter he is writing and reading it out load.

Val: Dear Father. I am sending word before me to ask that I might join you as a Benedictine brother. I have been well educated, particularly in the field of alchemy, and would like to join with you as one who would study and be a man of God. I will be arriving in a few days after you receive this letter, after a short stop and some business in Venice. Then I will be yours, and ready to devote myself to the Benedictine Order.

Valentine looks at the basil plant given to him by the friar and writes as he says the last line of the letter out load.

Val: Yours in God, Basil Valentine.

Valentine folds the letter and seals it and puts it in his pocket. He goes to the desk and picks up his bag. He blows out the candle, goes to the door looks around and exits.

The End

www.ingramcontent.com/pod-product-compliance
Lightning Source LLC
Chambersburg PA
CBHW052209090426
42741CB00010B/2471